21st Century Junior Library

Plants We Eat

by Jennifer Colby

CHERRY LAKE PUBLISHING * ANN ARBOR, MICHIGAN

CHERRY LAKE Publishing

Published in the United States of America by Cherry Lake Publishing
Ann Arbor, Michigan
www.cherrylakepublishing.com

Consultants: Elizabeth A. Glynn, Youth Education Coordinator, Matthaei Botanical Gardens and Nichols Arboretum, University of Michigan; Marla Conn, ReadAbility, Inc.

Photo Credits: © AdStock RF/Shutterstock Images, Cover, 4; © minadezhda/Shutterstock Images, 6; © Candace Hartley/Shutterstock Images, 8; © Brand X Pictures/Thinkstock, 10; © Kittikorn Phongok/Shutterstock Images, 12; © Fortish/Shutterstock Images, 14; © Alexander Kockin/Shutterstock Images, 16; © AGfoto/Shutterstock Images, 18; © watin/Shutterstock Images, 20

LIBRARY OF CONGRESS CATALOGING-IN-PUBLICATION DATA

Colby, Jennifer, 1971-
Plants we eat/by Jennifer Colby. - [Revised edition]
pages cm.—(21st century junior library)
Includes bibliographical references and index.
ISBN 978-1-63188-039-1—ISBN 978-1-63188-125-1—
ISBN 978-1-63188-082-7—ISBN 978-1-63188-168-8
1. Plants, Edible–Juvenile literature. I. Title. II. Series: 21st century junior library.
QK98.5.A1C65 2014
581.6'32–dc23 2014006193

Cherry Lake Publishing would like to acknowledge the work of The Partnership for 21st Century Skills. Please visit www.p21.org *for more information.*

Printed in the United States of America

CONTENTS

How many of these fruits or vegetables
do you eat?

Where Does Food Come From?

Do you buy most of your food from a grocery store? Did you know that many foods are grown on farms? **Vegetables** are grown on farms.

Vegetables are plants that people can eat. Many foods are made from plants. Let's take a look at the plants people eat.

Cereal is made from grains of plants like wheat, rice, oats, and corn.

Cereals and breads are made from different kinds of **grains**. Grains are the seeds of plants. Grains are grown on farms, too.

Make a Guess!

Think about a piece of pizza. Guess what kinds of plants were used to make the crust. How about the toppings? Have an adult help you find the answers online. Were your guesses correct?

The leaves of these vegetables have an important job to do. You can eat these leaves.

Sun Food

Something wonderful happens every day with plants. Plants collect water through their **roots**. Their leaves take in air and sunlight. Plants use the water, air, and sunlight to make their own food. This is called **photosynthesis**.

The parts of a plant work together to grow fruit and make seeds.

Sunlight gives a plant energy to make food. The food gives the plant energy to grow. The plant uses the energy from food to grow more **roots**, **stems**, and leaves. The plant also uses the energy from food to make flowers. **Fruit** grows from the plant's flowers. Inside the fruit are seeds. Inside each seed is a tiny plant. Fruit protects the new seeds of a plant.

You can eat many different plant parts. They give you energy to grow!

Do you eat broccoli? Guess what? You are eating a flower!

Good Enough to Eat

There are many kinds of **edible** plants in the world. Edible means safe to eat. Each vegetable has parts that are edible. Radishes are the roots of the plant. Asparagus is the stem of the plant. Potatoes are fat underground stems called **tubers**. Broccoli is the flower of the plant. Do you eat lettuce? You are eating the leaves of a plant!

Corn is a grain. Each kernel of corn has a seed inside.

The fruit of a plant can be edible. What is your favorite fruit? Is it an orange or a banana? A tomato is also a fruit. It has seeds inside. Some seeds are also edible.

Wheat, rice, and oats are grain plants. We eat their seeds. Corn is also a grain. Each corn **kernel** is a whole fruit with a seed inside.

Grains are a main source of food energy for people all over the world.

When you eat black pepper, you are eating the fruit of the plant.

We can make meals taste better with **spices** and **herbs**. Black pepper is a spice. It is the dried fruit of the plant. Cinnamon is a spice made from the bark of the plant. Mint is an herb that comes from the leaf of the plant.

Do you like to eat sweets things? Here's a surprise. The sugar in candy, cookies, and cakes comes from plants!

Ask Questions!

Visit your local grocery store. Talk to the person who takes care of the vegetables. Ask how many vegetables the store sells. Find a vegetable that you have never eaten before and ask for a taste!

Red peppers are the fruit of the plant. They have seeds inside. They can be eaten raw or cooked.

The Perfect Meal

Try cooking a meal that contains every different kind of plant part. Ask an adult to help you make a stir-fry. Start with carrots. They are roots. Red pepper is a fruit. It adds flavor and bright color. Bamboo shoots are a fun choice for stems. Add Napa cabbage leaves. Broccoli is a bunch of flowers. Snow peas add seeds to your dish.

A stir-fry can contain every plant part.

Chop up all of the vegetables. Then cook them with some oil in a skillet. Enjoy your delicious and healthy meal. You are eating every plant part!

Think!

Write down all of the vegetables your school offers for lunch next week. Put them in groups by colors. How many different colors did you eat? Eating many different colors of vegetables will help you stay healthy.

GLOSSARY

edible (ED-uh-buhl) something that is safe to eat

fruit (FROOT) the part of a plant that holds the seeds

grains (GREYNZ) seeds from plants like wheat, rice, oats, and corn that are used for food

herbs (URBZ) plants used in cooking

kernel (KUR-nl) a small, soft seed contained inside an single fruit

photosynthesis (foh-toh-SIN-thi-sis) the process of using light energy to combine air and water to make a plant's food

roots (ROOTS) underground parts of plants that store plant food

spices (SPYES-ez) plant parts with a strong smell or taste used to flavor food

stems (STEMZ) the long parts of plants from which leaves and flowers grow

tubers (TOO-berz) fat, underground stems that store plant food

vegetables (VEJ-tuh-buhlz) plants grown to be eaten

FIND OUT MORE

BOOKS

Kenin, Justine, and Becky Lettenberger. *We Grew It—Let's Eat It!* Washington, DC: Tenley Circle Press, 2010.

Zoehfeld, Kathleen Weidner, and Priscilla Lamont. *Secrets of the Garden: Food Chains and the Food Web in Our Backyard.* New York: Alfred A. Knopf, 2012.

WEB SITES

University of Illinois Extension—The Great Plant Escape: In Search of Green Life

http://urbanext.illinois.edu/gpe/case1/c1f.html

Try fun activities to learn how foods grow.

WGBH Educational Foundation—Supermarket Botany

www.pbslearningmedia.org/asset/lsps07_int_plantparts/

Match pictures of plants you find in the grocery store to the words describing the plant part.

INDEX

ABOUT THE AUTHOR

Jennifer Colby is a school librarian, and she also has a bachelor's degree in Landscape Architecture. By writing these books, she has combined her talents for two of her favorite things. She likes to garden and grow her own food. In June she makes strawberry jam for her children to enjoy all year long.